Greetings From

SENILITY

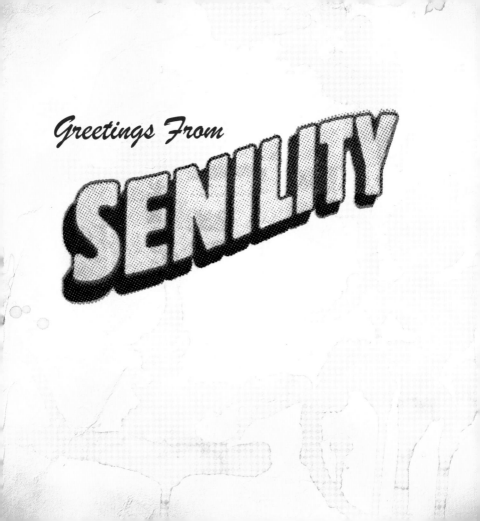

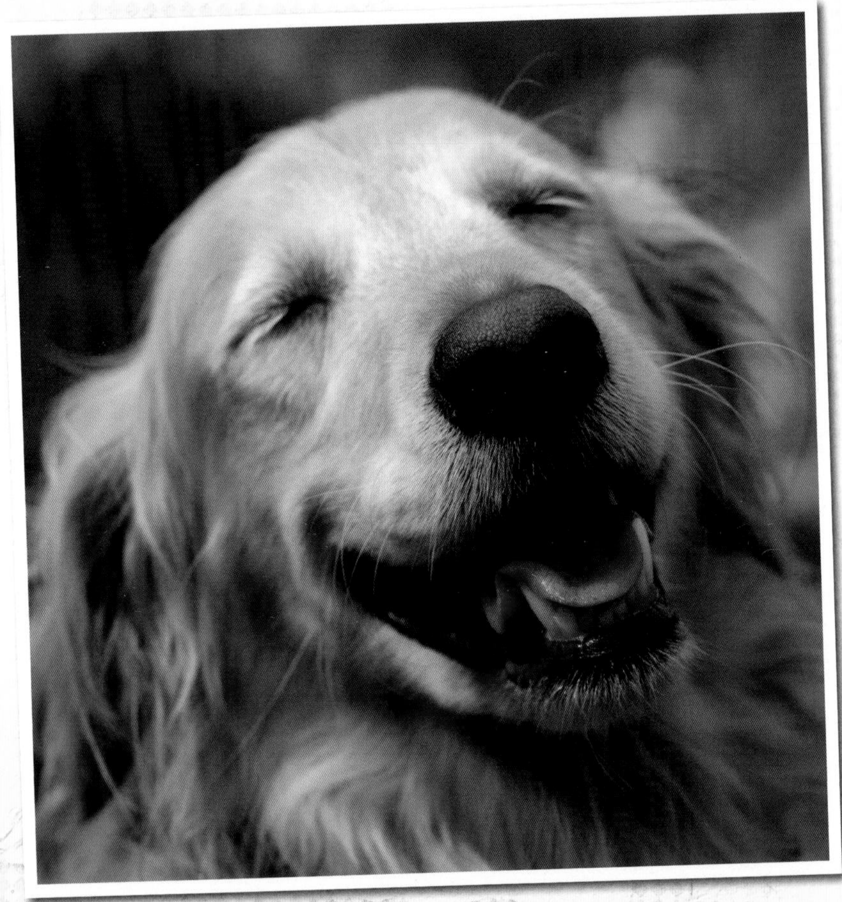

Greetings From

SENILITY

Your Road Map to Aging

■ WILLOW CREEK PRESS®

Published by Willow Creek Press, Inc.
P.O. Box 147, Minocqua, Wisconsin 54548

Photo Credits:

p2 © Horst Herget/Masterfile; p8 © Minden Pictures/Masterfile; p11 © Artiga Photo/Masterfile;
p12 © Minden Pictures/Masterfile; p15 © Minden Pictures/Masterfile; p20 © F. Lukasseck/Masterfile;
p23 © Minden Pictures/Masterfile; p24 © Minden Pictures/Masterfile;
p28 © Minden Pictures/Masterfile; p31 © Thomas Kokta/Masterfile; p35 © Marie Blum/Masterfile;
p39 © Steve Craft/Masterfile; p40 © Photoshot/Masterfile; p43 © Robert Harding Images/Masterfile;
p44 © Frank Krahmer/Masterfile; p47 © Minden Pictures/Masterfile; p48 © Minden Pictures/Masterfile;
p52 © Jeremy Woodhouse/Masterfile; p55 © Photoshot/Masterfile; p59 © F. Lukasseck/Masterfile;
p60 © Minden Pictures/Masterfile; p63 © David Mendelsohn/Masterfile;
p64 © Minden Pictures/Masterfile; p67 © Artiga Photo/Masterfile; p68 © Greg Stott/Masterfile;
p75 © Ken & Michelle Dyball/Masterfile; p76 © Minden Pictures/Masterfile;
p80 © Gary Gerovac/Masterfile; p83 © Photoshot/Masterfile; p87 © Minden Pictures/Masterfile;
p88 © UpperCut Images/Masterfile; p91 © Minden Pictures/Masterfile;
p95 © Minden Pictures/Masterfile;

Design: Donnie Rubo
Printed in Canada

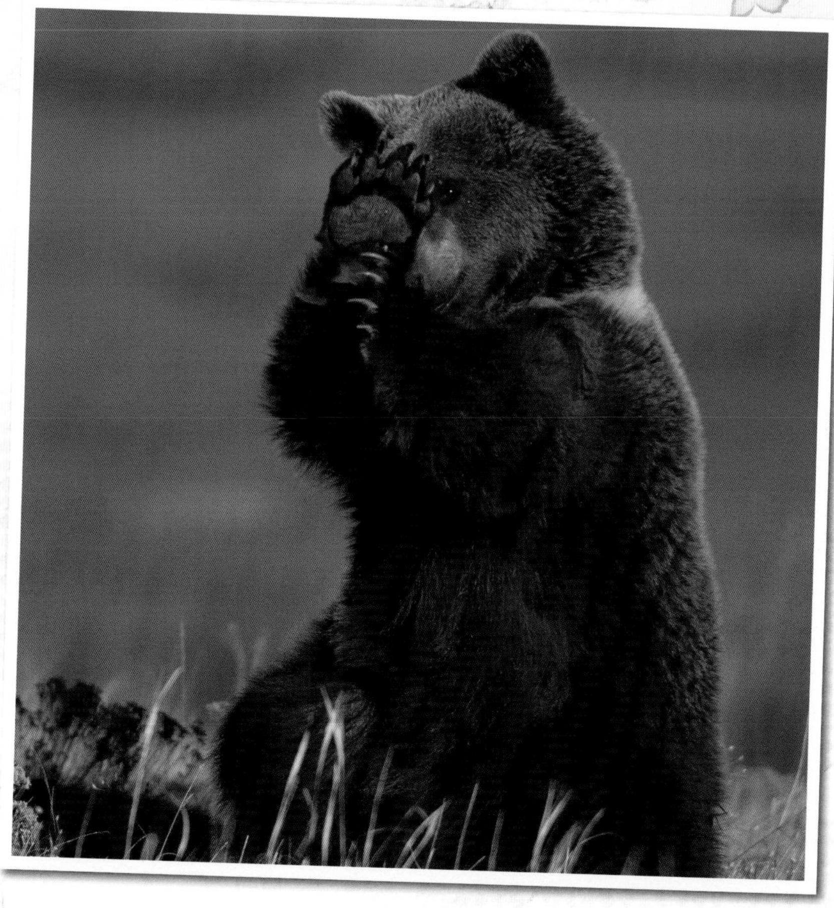

The short, sweet season of youth seemed to you an eternity. You couldn't wait to put it behind you, to grow up, to graduate from a bike to a car.

"There is always one moment in childhood
when the door opens and lets the future in."

—Deepak Chopra

"In dog years I should already be dead."

—Unknown

Well, you got your wish,
and soon you were careening
down the highway of life,
your startling progress
measured by benchmark birthdays
whizzing past like so many
mile-markers: 21 - 30 - 40...

Where is it all headed?

Fact is, you're driving a
pre-owned vehicle once
possessed and often mistreated
by your childhood, adolescence,
and your adulthood.

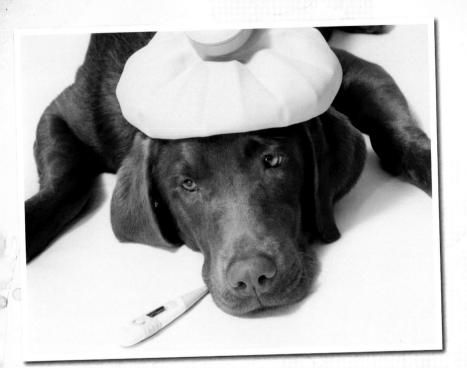

"It's not the pace of life that concerns me,
it's the sudden stop at the end."

—Unknown

"But I have promises to keep,
and miles to go before I sleep."

–Robert Frost

Although your warranty has expired,
with careful driving, regular
maintenance, and reading these
ABC's of Aging, you can expect
the road to stretch on indefinitely.

So slow down for once and
start enjoying the scenery.

"Funny, I don't remember being absentminded."

—Unknown

ABSENTMINDEDNESS DR.

"If all is not lost, where is it?"

—Unknown

"It well becomes those who are no longer
young to forget they ever were."

–Seigneur de Saint-Evremond, 1696

"I still have a full deck; I just shuffle slower now."

—Unknown

ACCEPTANCE AVE.

"I didn't get old on purpose, it just happened.
If you're lucky, it could happen to you."

–Andy Rooney

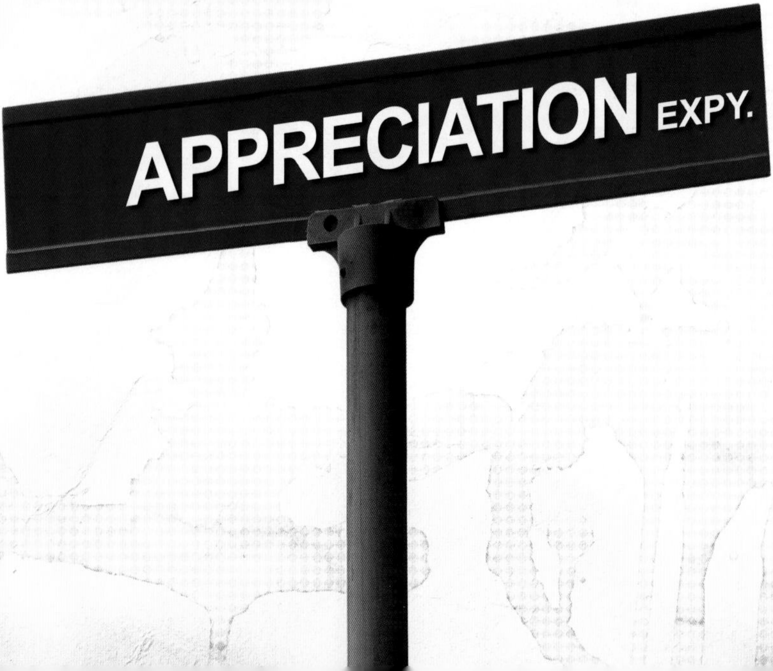
APPRECIATION EXPY.

"Grow old with me! The best is yet to be."

–Robert Browning

"The other day a man asked me what I thought
was the best time of my life. 'Why,'
I answered without a thought, 'now.'"

–David Grayson

"You are as young as your faith, as old as your doubt;
as young as your self-confidence, as old as your fear;
as young as your hope, as old as your despair."

–Douglas MacArthur

ATTITUDE LN.

"I don't do alcohol anymore—
I get the same effect just standing up."

–Unknown

BALANCE ST.

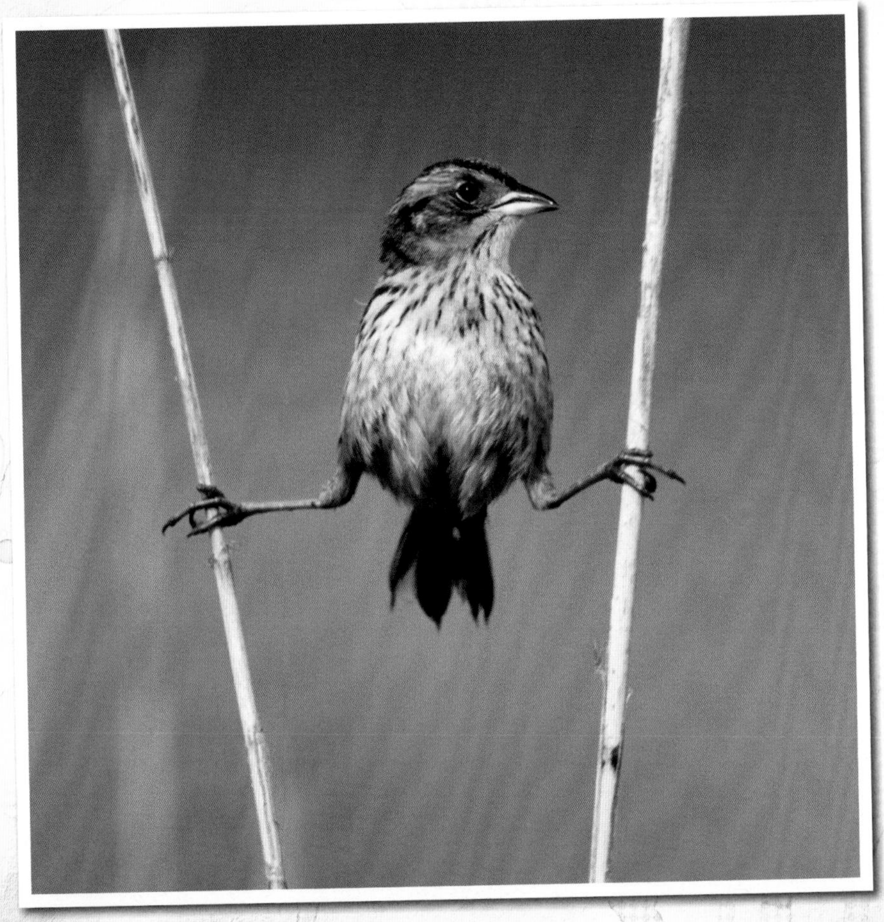

"The great secret that all old people share is that you really haven't changed in seventy or eighty years. Your body changes, but you don't change at all. And that, of course, causes great confusion."

–Doris Lessing

"Inside every older person is a younger person wondering what happened."

–Jennifer Yane

CONFUSION ALY.

"Anyone who stops learning is old, whether at twenty or eighty."

–Henry Ford

CURIOSITY JCT.

"Morality comes with the sad wisdom of age,
when the sense of curiosity has withered."

–Graham Greene

"Every one desires to live long, but no one would be old."

-Jonathan Swift

"I refuse to admit that I am more than fifty-two, even if that does make my sons illegitimate."

–*Nancy Astor*

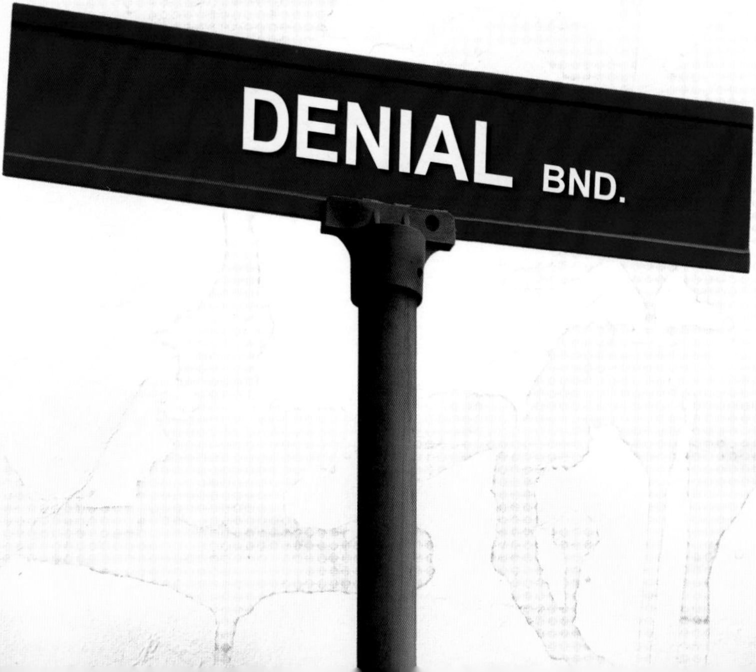
DENIAL BND.

"Middle age is when you choose your
cereal for the fiber, not the toy."

–Unknown

"When did my wild oats turn to prunes and All Bran?"

–Unknown

"Dreams are renewable. No matter what our age
or condition, there are still untapped possibilities
within us and new beauty waiting to be born."

–Dale E. Turner

"In a dream you are never eighty."

—Anne Sexton

DREAMS LN.

"You know you've reached middle age when a doctor, not a policeman, tells you to slow down."

–Unknown

DRIVING CIR.

"I want to die peacefully in my sleep like my grandfather,
not kicking and screaming like the passengers in his car."

–Unknown

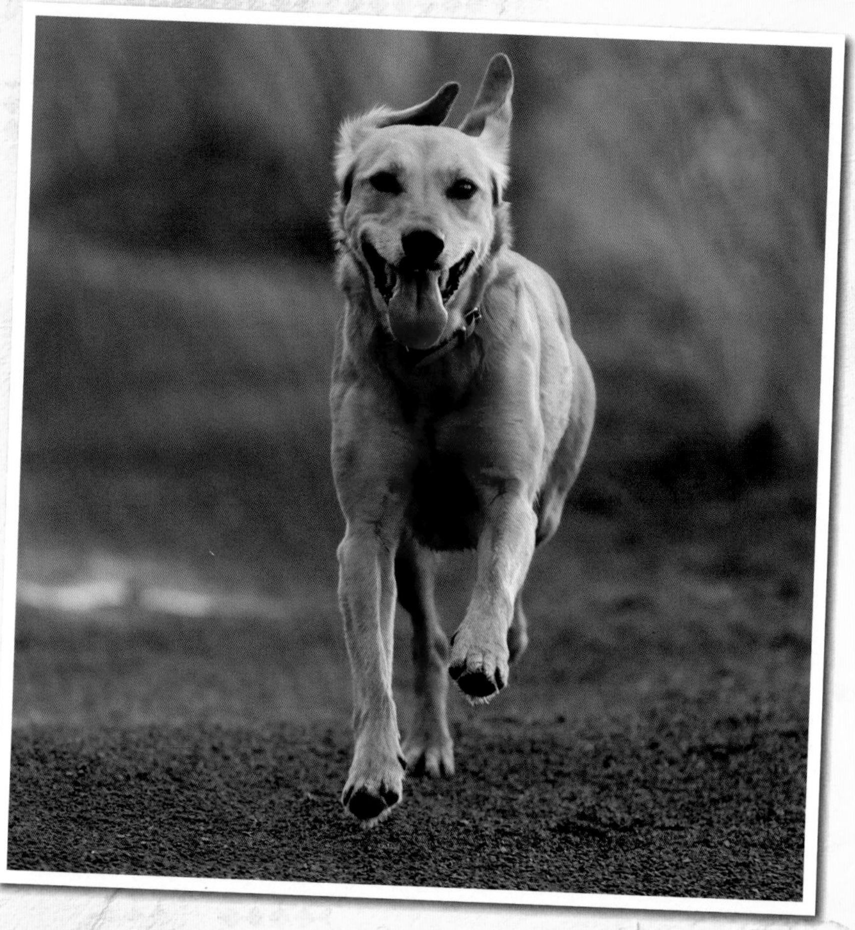

"None are so old as those who have outlived enthusiasm."

–Henry David Thoreau

Here's the good news: your eyes
won't get too much worse."

—Unknown

"I am getting to the age when I can only enjoy the last sport left. It is called hunting for your spectacles."

—Edward Gray

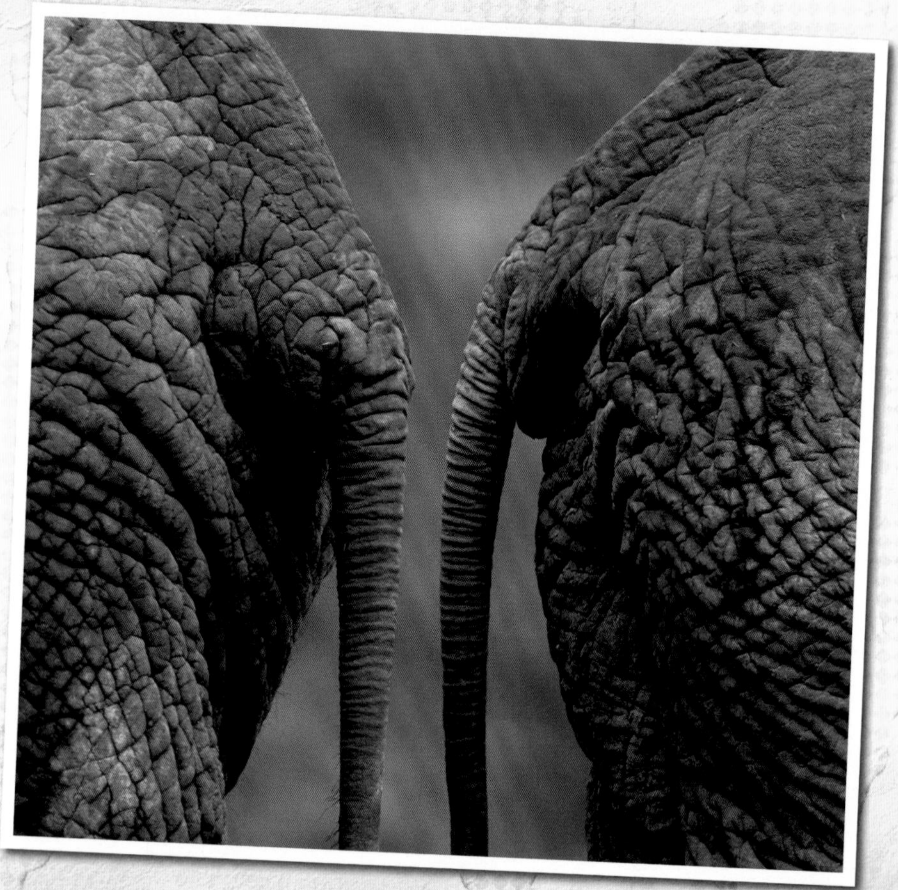

"I'm learning to multi-task as I age. For instance, yesterday I sneezed and farted at the same time."

—Unknown

FLATULENCE PASS

"First you forget names, then you forget faces, then you forget to pull your zipper up, then you forget to pull your zipper down."

–Leo Rosenberg

FORGETFULNESS CIR.

"At least your secrets are safe with your friends because they can't remember them anyway."

—Unknown

"When grace is joined with wrinkles, it is adorable.
There is an unspeakable dawn in happy old age."

–Victor Hugo

"Beautiful young people are accidents of nature,
but beautiful old people are works of art."

–Eleanor Roosevelt

"The simplest toy, one which even the youngest child can operate, is called a grandparent."

–Sam Levenson

GRANDPARENTHOOD LN.

"Grandchildren are God's way of
compensating us for growing old."

-Mary H. Waldrip

"There is only one cure for gray hair. It was invented
by a Frenchman. It is called the guillotine."

-P.G. Wodehouse

"It is not by the gray of the hair that one knows the age of the heart."

–Edward Bulwer-Lytton

GRAYING BLVD.

"They talk about the economy this year.
Hey, my hairline is in recession... I'm in a depression."

–Rick Majerus

HAIR LOSS DR.

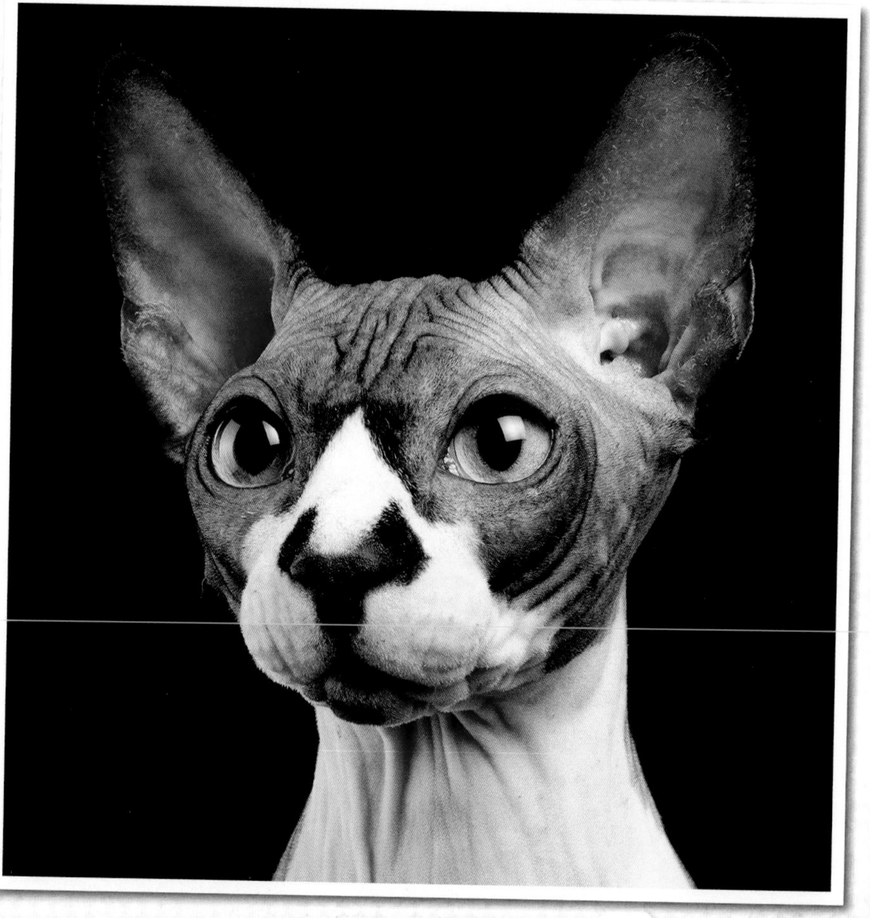

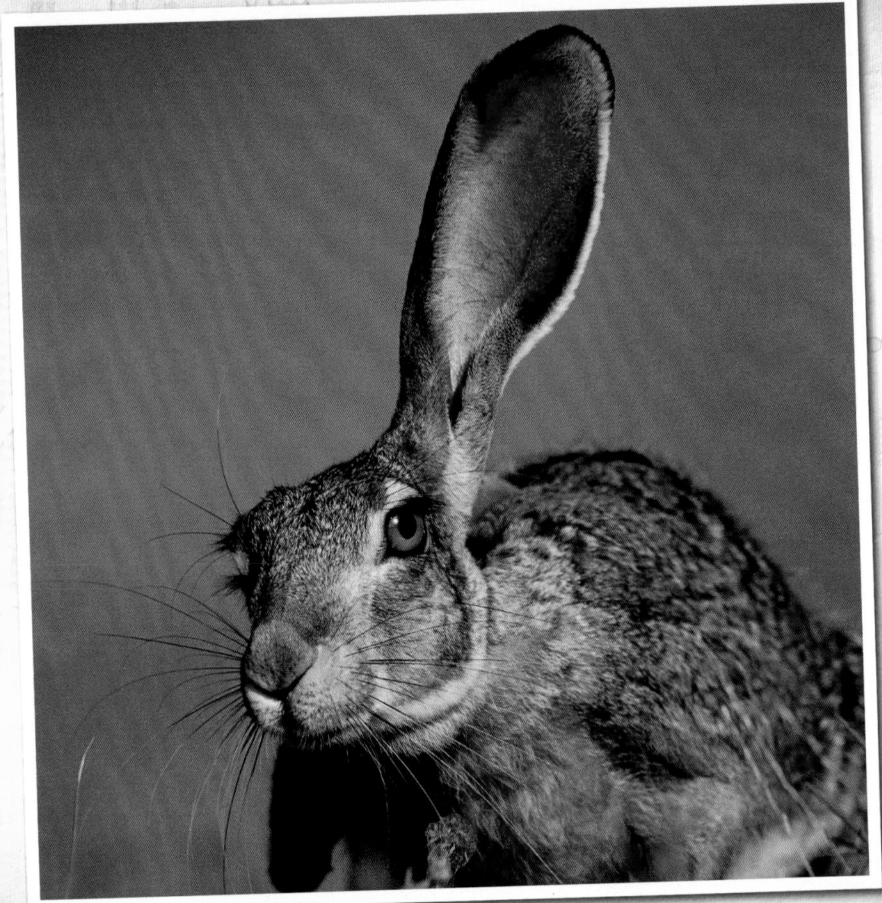

An elderly gentleman proudly states to his friend
that, although his new, state-of-the-art hearing aid
was very expensive, it was worth every penny.
"What kind is it?" Asked the friend.
"Nine-thirty," answered the gentleman.

—Unknown

HEARING LOSS AVE.

"If you live to be one hundred, you've got it made.
Very few people die past that age."

–George Burns

Middle age is the time when a man is always thinking
that in a week or two he will feel as good as ever."

—Don Marquis

"Middle age is when a narrow waist and
a broad mind begin to change places."

—Unknown

"The denunciation of the young is a necessary part of the hygiene of older people, and greatly assists the circulation of the blood."

–Logan Pearsall Smith

INTOLERANCE DR.

"Don't let aging get you down. It's too hard to get back up."

–John Wagner

JOINTS BND.

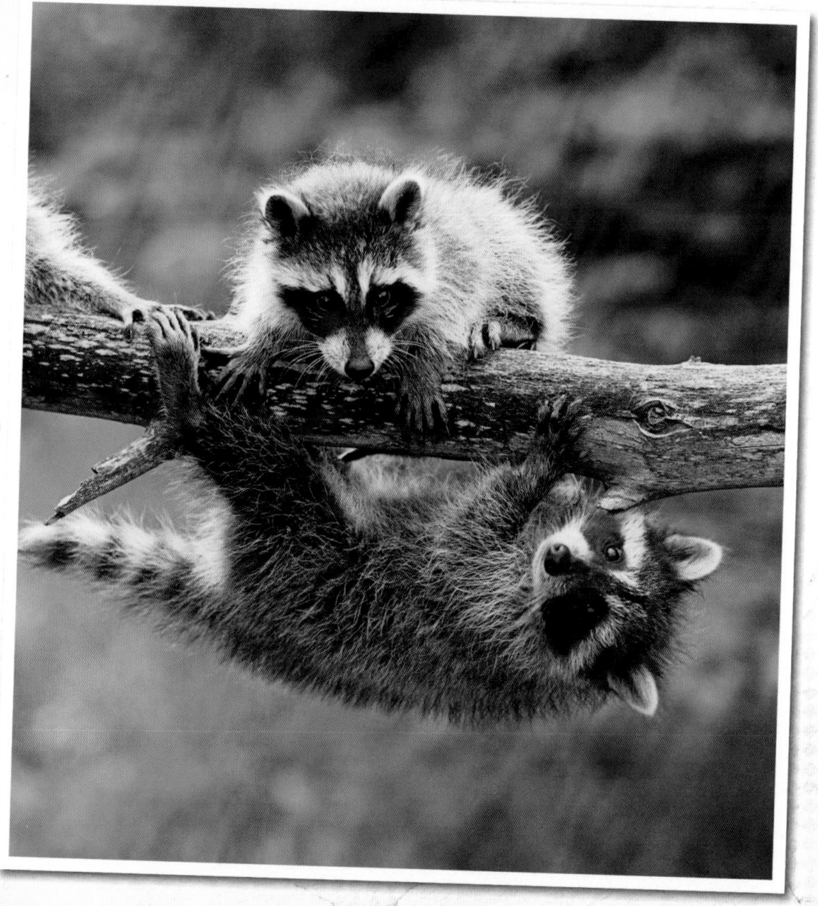

"My mother-in-law had a pain beneath her left breast. Turned out to be a trick knee."

–Phyllis Diller

"Take care of your knees while you're still young—you'll miss them one day."

—Unknown

"Never under any circumstances take a sleeping pill and a laxative on the same night."

–Dave Barry

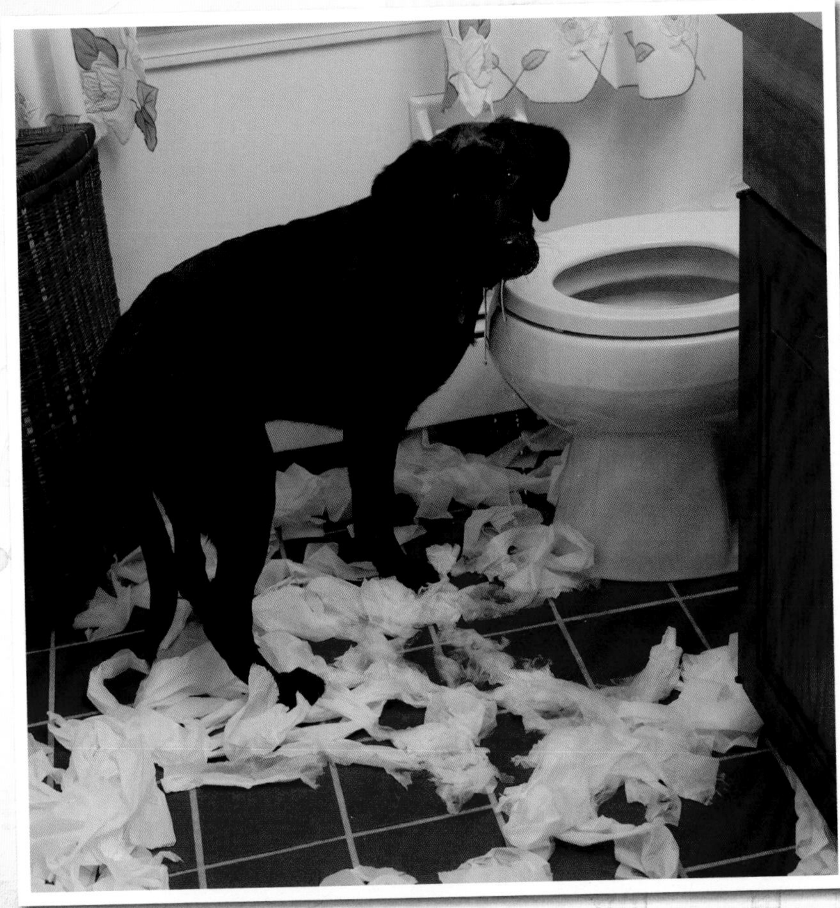

"The process of maturing is an art to be learned, an effort
to be sustained. By the age of fifty you have made yourself
what you are, and if it is good, it is better than your youth."

—Marya Mannes

"Everything slows down with age, except the time it takes cake and ice cream to reach your hips."

–John Wagner

MATURITY ST.

"Middle age is when a guy keeps turning off lights for economical rather than romantic reasons."

–Lillian Carter

"Inflation is when you pay fifteen dollars for the ten-dollar haircut you used to get for five dollars when you had hair."

-Sam Ewing

"It was all so different before everything changed."

—Unknown

"Adulthood is when the ghosts of childhood appear."

—Holden Rinehart

NOSTALGIA ISLE.

"How old would you be if you didn't know how old you are?"

–Satchel Paige

OPTIMISM CIR.

"You can't help getting older, but you don't have to get old."

–George Burns

"Old age is an excellent time for outrage. My goal is to say or do at least one outrageous thing every week."

–Louis Kronenberger

"There was no respect for youth when I was young,
and now that I am old, there is no respect for age—
I missed it coming and going."

-J.B. Priestly

OUTRAGE WAY

"Age is something impressive, it sums up one's life: maturity reached slowly and against many obstacles, illnesses cured, griefs and despairs overcome, and unconscious risks taken; maturity formed through so many desires, hopes, regrets, forgotten things, loves. Age represents a fine cargo of experiences and memories."

—Antoine de Saint-Exupery

PRIDE DR.

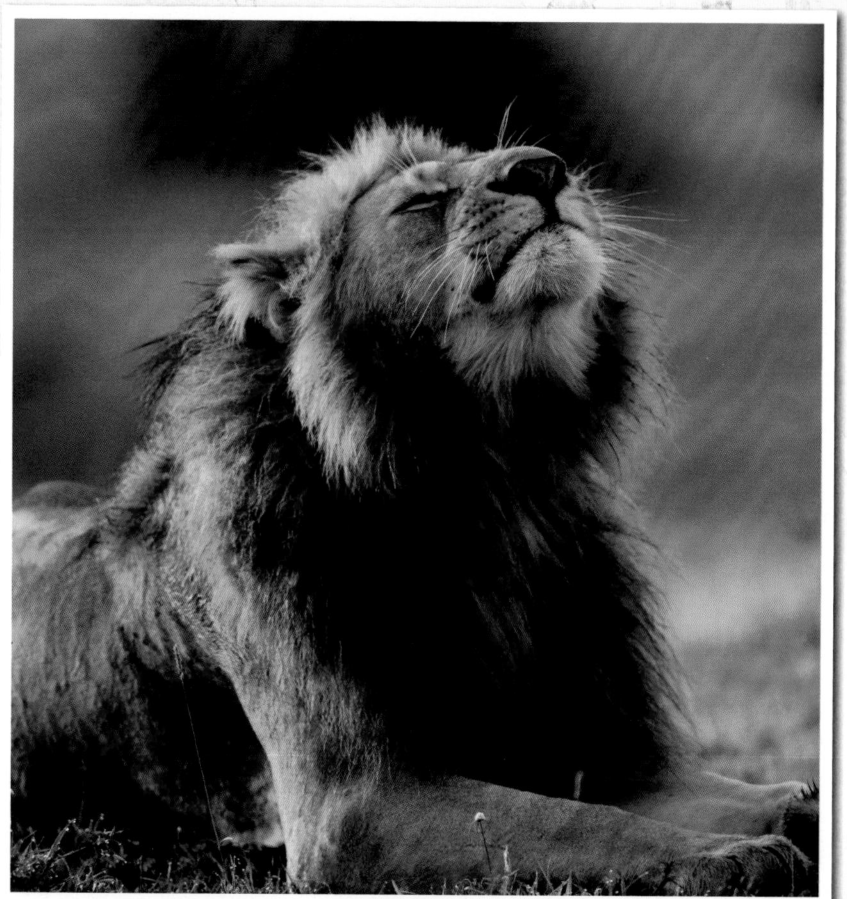

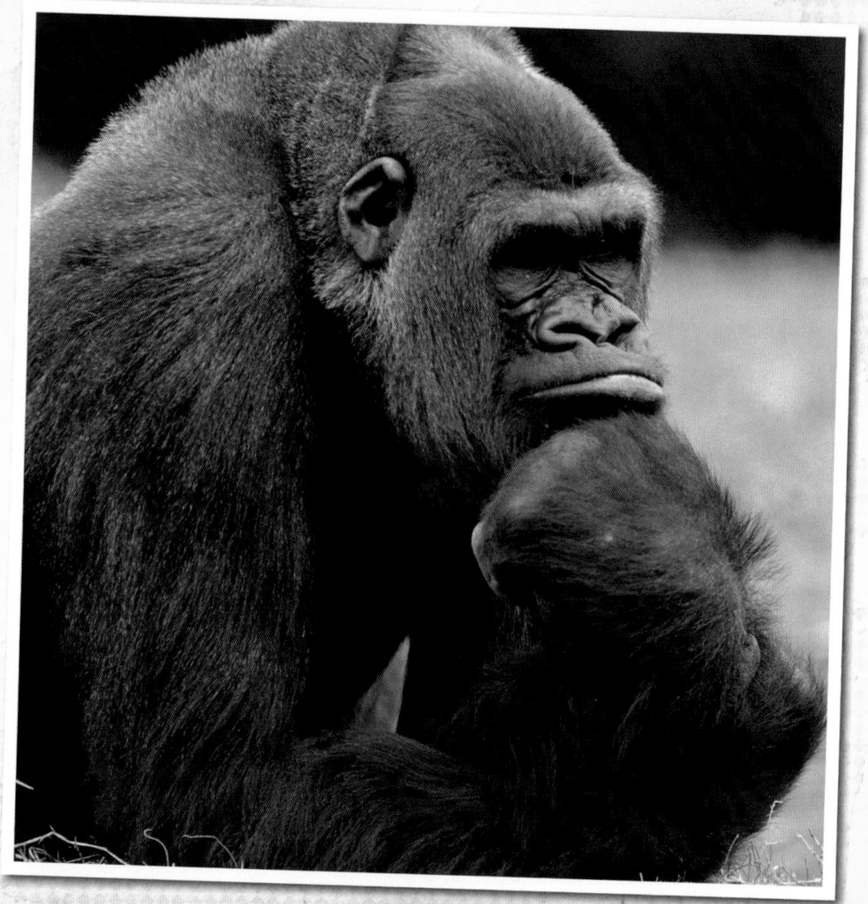

"It's hard to feel middle-aged, because how can you tell how long you are going to live?"

–Mignon McLaughlin

QUESTIONING AVE.

"Age does not diminish the extreme disappointment of having a scoop of ice cream fall from the cone."

–Jim Fiebig

"Do not regret getting older.
It is a privilege denied to many."

–Unknown

"When you become senile, you won't know it."

–Bill Cosby

"When I was young I was called a rugged individualist.
When I was in my fifties I was considered eccentric.
Here I am doing and saying the same things
I did then and I'm labeled senile."

–George Burns

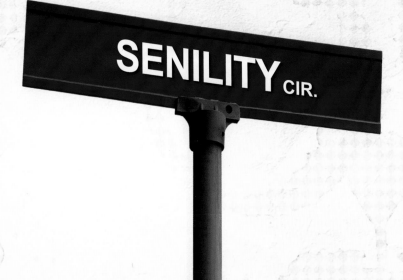

SENILITY CIR.

"A person is always startled when he hears himself called old for the first time."

–Oliver Wendell Holmes

SURPRISE ST.

"Old age is the most unexpected of
all things that happen to a man."

-Leon Trotsky

"When our vices desert us, we flatter
ourselves that we are deserting our vices."

–Francois Duc de La Rochefoucauld

"Don't worry about avoiding temptation—
as you grow older, it starts avoiding you."

—Unknown

TEMPTATION LN.

"Age attacks when we least expect it."

–Carrie Latet

UNPREPAREDNESS AVE.

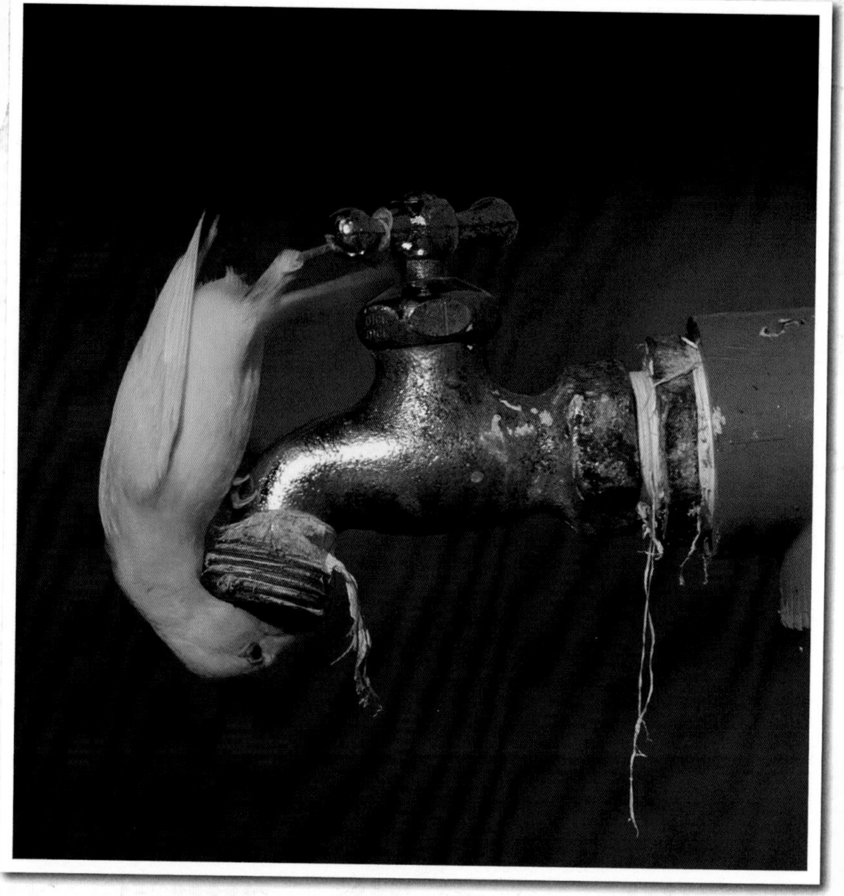

"I can remember when the air was clean and sex was dirty."

–George Burns

"I'm taking Viagra and drinking prune juice.
I don't know whether I'm coming or going."

-Rodney Dangerfield

VIAGRA LN.

"Wisdom doesn't necessarily come with age.
Sometimes age just shows up all by itself."

–Tom Wilson

"The older I grow the more I distrust the familiar doctrine that age brings wisdom."

–H.L. Mencken

"There is always a lot to be thankful for, if you take the time to look. For example, I'm sitting here thinking how nice it is that wrinkles don't hurt."

—Unknown

"Time might be a great healer, but it's a lousy beautician."

—Unknown

WRINKLES JCT.

"If you carry your childhood with you,
you never become older."

–Tom Stoppard

YOUTHFULNESS EXPY.

"It is never too late to have a happy childhood."

-Tom Robbins.

"We do not quit playing because we grow old;
we grow old because we quit playing."

–Oliver Wendell Holmes